LETTERS TO
VIRGINIA WOOLF

Lisa Williams

Hamilton Books
A member of
The Rowman & Littlefield Publishing Group
Lanham · Boulder · New York · Toronto · Oxford

Copyright © 2005 by
Hamilton Books
4501 Forbes Boulevard
Suite 200
Lanham, Maryland 20706
Hamilton Books Acquisitions Department (301) 459-3366

PO Box 317
Oxford
OX2 9RU, UK

Library of Congress Control Number: 2005922592
ISBN 0-7618-3205-X (paperback : alk. ppr.)

For my Mother, Charlotte

And for my dear departed friend, Charlotte.

Contents

Acknowledgments

Many people made the writing of this book possible. I want to thank Ramapo College of New Jersey, The Writer's Room in New York City, and New York University's Faculty Resource Network for their generous support. Charlotte Ann Frick generously read this manuscript and gave me invaluable comments in the midst of her fight to survive an insidious and invasive spread of cancer. I am so appreciative to Chella Courington for reading through many drafts of this book. Jane Marcus and Tuzyline Jita Allan are a constant source of inspiration to me. I also want to thank Rika Lesser and the members of the 92nd St. Y's master poetry class for giving me such helpful comments on my poems. I'm grateful for my wonderful mother and brothers. My husband Richard is constantly there supporting me, and my son Sammy always brings a deep joy to my life.

Abbreviations

AROO	*A Room of One's Own*
D	*The Diary of Virginia Woolf*
MD	*Mrs. Dalloway*
TL	*To the Lighthouse*
TG	*Three Guineas*

Part I

"Yes, the chimneys and the coast-guard unseen by any one make one remember the overpowering sorrow. And what can this sorrow be?"

Jacob's Room 49

"Back and back we are drawn to steep ourselves in what, perhaps, is only an image of the reality, not the reality itself, a summer's day, imagined in the heart of a northern winter."

"On Not Knowing Greek" 35

Dear Virginia Woolf,

I can hear your words, "A common interest unites us; it is one world, one life" (*Three Guineas* 142). You had a vision of a world without war. And your words waft up now from layers and layers of sorrow.

For we all recall over and over again that crisp fall day. The cloudless sky that day did not beckon the dead to sing or the living to fall. Instead the sun seemed particularly fond of the children in the playground, as it guided the soap through the bubble-blower, and then made the many bubbles sparkle and glisten against the cool air. The sun teased the children, leading them on as they chased the yellow and blue-tinted bubbles rising in the air—bubbles that seemed to laugh with their ascent.

The children slid down sliding-ponds, climbed down monkey bars, and glided down poles with ease. And the slant of light that day lit up the reds and blues of the playground, light simmering into movement—light counting in rhythmic unity, one, two, three—one, two, three—catch me, catch me, if you can—one, two, three. The light teased us, teased us bad that day.

My son gathered leaves on the ground in a small, red bucket, collected fragments of sticks, and then watched the grains of sand fall through his fingers. He pointed up, up, up, to the trees, where the breeze was messing with the leaves. It had been only a month that he had begun walking. Max placed his hand in mine and we stepped up to the blue wheel, his favorite place to pretend he was a driver on a bus. Max turned and turned and turned the wheel, peering out at the children in the sandbox, as his future stretched endlessly ahead of him.

"Go tell Aunt Rhodie, Go tell Aunt Rhodie, Go tell Aunt Rhodie, the old gray goose is dead. The one she's been saving, the one she's been saving, the one she's been saving to make a feather bed." Old rhymes from my childhood seemed to rise up out of the air to form a circle round us, dancing. And now I wonder if the memory of this sad rhyme was part of the sorrow the sun so cleverly concealed from us.

With Max's hand in mine, I grew down, down, down, traveling backwards. Yes, I will be your guide, my steps told him; I will hold your hand, and together we will go a-walking this fall day, slowly making our way up steps.

But the moment was over so quickly. "A plane crashed into the World Trade Center," a babysitter said to me, as Max focused all of his energy on turning the blue wheel.

Her words did not register. How could a pilot manage to do something like that?

"How did such an accident occur?" I asked.

"I don't know."

The day still unfolded languidly in silent perfection. The babysitter's words made me sad as I thought of all those people on that plane. Whose mistake had it been? But the day still attested to the enduring presence of the living. The light danced down the pavement, made the flowers yawn lazily. And the children rejoiced there was no need to sing, "Rain, rain, go away, come again another day."

When I got home to give Max his morning nap, the phone began to ring. As the world shattered into many pieces, he continued to dream, nestled peacefully in a pocket of sleep.

"Is Jeff all right? Did you hear what happened? A plane crashed into the World Trade Center." One by one the questions came.

I went to call him, but suddenly the phone was dead, so I got my cell phone, but that was dead too. I found myself surrounded by caves of silence. All of New York had become eerily quiet.

I turned the TV on. And there were the images that have become so familiar to us all now—a plane headed right into the majestic building, and then the debris began to fall, and a shower of yellow and red flames raced up the tower, devouring all those people trapped inside, behind those windows and walls.

What followed seemed like part of a sci-fi movie. Sometimes it seemed as if the laws of gravity were suspended, and I was walking slowly on air towards an unknown destination, trying as hard as I could to get my legs back to the floor. But it was not possible. In other moments life speeded up, and time was moving as if someone had pressed the fast-forward button. I couldn't catch up with my own movements propelling me forward.

My husband was working five blocks away. I turned the number over in my mind and examined it. Five blocks should be far enough away. But then the thought turned into its opposite, and I could only ask, but what if it's not. I tried the phone again, but it was still dead. The silence was everywhere.

Suddenly there was noise again. The phone rang.

"I'm okay," he said.

I couldn't find any words. Short and staccato sounds fell from me. I was frozen. I couldn't feel.

Jeff told me he was going to walk home from there. He was on his way out of his building. Once we hung up, the phones were dead once again. And I had forgotten to tell him that I loved him.

"The second tower of the World Trade Center has fallen," the TV anchor reported. I saw the black dust falling, filling the air like a vacuum cleaner going in reverse, emptying its tiny particles of debris everywhere.

I couldn't push the panic away anymore.

What if he's on the street now? Could he survive something like that if he was blocks away on the street when this happened? How does a hundred story building manage to fall? Where would it land? What would it cover, or demolish?

About an hour later, the phone managed to ring again.

"I'm okay. I didn't end up leaving," Jeff said.

And this time I didn't forget to tell him.

"I love you too. You can't believe what it's like down here. I opened the door to go out and all I could see was people running and blackness everywhere. I've never been so scared in my life. And now everyone's leaving to go uptown now. It's gonna take me awhile."

"Just get here."

"It's gonna take me hours to get home. But do me a favor. Go out and get some money. And some water and milk. Who knows what's gonna happen. You can't believe what it's like down here."

The walking would be long. First past those narrow winding streets where once cows had grazed long ago, and then up past Union Square and Grand Central, and then still there would be another couple of miles to cover.

I scooped Max into his carriage and we went down, down, down the elevator and out onto the street.

There were no cars on the streets—only hordes of people rushing as quickly as possible, stepping with large movements, as if that might control the panic now everywhere.

The line at the bank stretched down the block. Everyone had the same thought. Get money. And so Max and I waited, dumb and numb like the others. The sun, now hot, now overhead, seemed to laugh at our stupidity from far away.

When we entered the supermarket, the lines at the cash register circled round the store. I couldn't deal with it. Across the street at the health food store, for ten cents more, I could buy water and milk. Hardly anyone was there.

When I got back to our apartment building, I noticed my neighbor, a very pregnant woman, sitting on a beach chair. The baby inside seemed to prance across her belly, while beads of sweat formed on her forehead.

"I sure hope it's not today," she said. It's any day now. But I hope it's not today."

"The hospitals will be busy," I said, not knowing then how few people would make it there. All those doctors, nurses, medics, waiting and waiting that day for the people to arrive who had already perished.

I looked at her round, large belly, and her tired, frightened eyes. And yet we could not speak of it. We had no words. We created, instead, fragments of conversation, until finally, from down the block, I could see Jeff walking slowly towards us.

He was in front of me, but he had not yet returned. His black pants were covered with white soot. His shirtsleeves were rolled up to his elbows, and grime and sweat formed a layer over his skin and clothes. When I saw him, I knew then he had been to a remote place, a place where I could never enter.

I was hugging him, but he wasn't there yet.

"This was the worst day of my life." Jeff's voice broke into nervous laughter.

"I can imagine," Lorraine paused for a moment and then added. "I just hope it's not today," she said and looked at her belly.

"The hospitals will be busy enough," Jeff said.

He was starting to crumble, I felt. I had to get him inside. The white debris covering his black pants made Jeff look like a moonwalker.

I wrapped my arm around Lorraine, leaned into the beach chair, and smelled the sweat down her arms and face. We still could not speak of it.

"Please let us know as soon as the big moment happens."

Lorraine nodded.

And we walked away.

I placed one arm in Jeff's and steered the stroller with the other one, as we walked slowly up the steps into the apartment building, and made our way to the elevator that took us to our floor.

Once we got inside, Jeff plopped down on the couch. His body seemed to disintegrate into many small parts.

"You can't imagine it," he said and closed his eyes. He was going to a place very far away.

"Da da. Da da. Da da," Max chirped. "Da da."

"You need to get out of here." I could feel his body splitting into fractured parts. "Will you come with us to the playground?" I suggested desperately.

"No. I can't. I just can't right now."

"Da da. Da da." Max pulled on his sleeve.

"I just can't." Jeff's voice was faint, barely audible.

"Just come with me." I paused for a few minutes and watched Jeff sink into the beige couch. I had to prevent his body from becoming undone. His legs looked like two spools of thread that were rapidly unraveling.

"Please. Just sit there instead. You don't have to do anything. Just be with us."

"Okay, Okay. But I'm not doing anything. I'm dead. I'm just too dead," he repeated wearily.

He walked behind us those three blocks to the park, like a soldier who had just gotten back from the war and could not speak of all he had seen.

Outside, the lighthearted laughter of children flooded the playground. One by one parents brought their children here. As they sat on benches, some waited for more news from those they had not yet heard from today, while others just waited for any kind of news. We all, that day, began a very long ritual of waiting.

Shovels gleefully scooped up pockets of sand, and small bodies slid down sliding-ponds. There was so much to discover. Jeff sat back on a bench by himself, and I took Max's hand, as we walked together into the sandbox to join the others. There was little space left for us to sit, but we found a spot just big enough for the two of us to start our important work of filling our bucket with the millions and millions of grains of sand. The future continued to stretch on and on endlessly before us, but for me it no longer unraveled effortlessly like the grains of sand dropping into Max's bucket. The future would be forever stained by the vision of those flames devouring the World Trade Center towers, those flames burning up those lives ended so abruptly, robbed of the future that was due them.

And yet it was the children that day who took a defiant stance against terror. While the rest of us waded through a vague and undetermined sense of dread, the children played on, refusing for now, to give up their short-lived innocence.

Dear Virginia Woolf,

Today, as I stroll around the streets of New York City, I think of your shell-shocked warrior, Septimus, from *Mrs. Dalloway*. He returned home from World War I, alone and bereft, wishing he could have simply refused to witness the bomb shatter and kill his friend instantaneously.

Septimus solved the whole problem by simply not feeling. I can hear him wondering "why he could see through bodies, see into the future when dogs will become men? . . . Scientifically speaking, the flesh was melted off the world. His body was macerated until only the nerve fibres were left" (MD 102-3).

We all stopped feeling for awhile, and just moved from one destination to another, like robots, going only where we needed to go.

Those days after September 11 were strange. It was as if the very structure of the cosmos had been altered. In the middle of January, the temperature would rise to seventy degrees, and we would shed our heavy clothes and walk with a simple sweater in Central Park. The ducks in the ponds still begged for food, and the barren trees seemed ready to produce new leaves. Then it would get colder for a while, and then without any notice warmer once again. Most of that winter seemed more like fall. It was as if that brisk September day lived on; it could not disappear, but would return again to remind us all that something had been irrevocably altered.

As I walked along the grass, and passed Central Park's large, majestic trees, and Max gathered leaves carefully into his toy stroller, I could hear your words, Virginia Woolf: "Then again silence fell; and then, night after night, sometimes in plain mid-day when the roses were bright and light turned on the wall its shape clearly there seemed to drop into this silence, this indifference, this integrity, the thud of something falling" (TL114). And yet though almost everything in New York City looked the same, beneath the surface it was all in disarray. We had no words for the emptiness. Surrounding us all were always the sounds and images of those towers, those lives, that had fallen.

At night I would stare and stare at my sleeping son, his small body curled into an arc. His head made his teddy bear a pillow. He still sucked happily on his pacifier. If it were not for him, I may not have known that beauty still existed in the world. I stood over him, watching him sleeping, sleeping, sleeping through it all.

Dear Virginia Woolf,

You asked women to form a society of outsiders to oppose war. I can hear your words today: "As a woman I have no country. As a woman I want no country. As a woman my country is the whole world" (TG 109).

I have been there Virginia, to Monk's House, your summer home. I have journeyed there to retrace the life you dared to live. As I looked in on your narrow, single bed, I remembered how you wrote that you never succeeded in writing about the body. As I stared into your room from behind the rope, I was struck by the chaste and monastic life you did lead, a life devoted to the arduous task of creating words to name the silences of women's lives. There, in your room, is just that bed, a simple dresser, a chair.

Outside the flowers bloomed. Words seemed to rise up from the soil, mixing with the earthy garden smells.

I walked over to the separate cinder building that was your study. Again, a rope prevented me from entering, but when I peered inside, I found a bare room with a large desk looking out on fields of grass where cows nibbled peacefully. Except for a black trunk behind the desk, the room was empty. It was the discipline you craved, Virginia. Stripped of worldly possessions, you entered this room with just your writing materials, and dipped your pen into the past, where you recreated with language the scenes of your childhood.

Outside your writing room, I looked far out into the fields where hills and sky blended peacefully together, wanting to know what did you see as you stared out of the window with your notebook and pen in hand.

How did you deal with all those losses? At thirteen, your mother dying suddenly, and then only two short years later, your half-sister too died, followed by your brother. With words creating elegy, you resurrected them from the dead, as their voices filled your pages.

I imagined you at thirteen years old, standing over your mother's bed as she lay dying. You stood with the others, listening to her voice grow more faint, her irregular breathing slowed down to a stop, but before that moment, there were her last words, "Hold yourself straight, my little goat" ("A Sketch" 84), she whispered before she left you.

I hated to leave your summer home, but dusk had arrived and the colors in your garden became slender in the fading sun. Your home, now a museum, was closing; down the road I could hear a dog barking, barking, barking, as if to bring an end to the day, now slipping away.

Dear Virginia Woolf,

I have retraced the steps you took, Virginia, from Monk's House to the river on the very last day of your life. The sun, the day I came, seemed to stretch her arms languorously over hills and streams, while the dirt from the road dissolved into granules of sand falling always just ahead of me, forming circles of dust landing on my arms and legs. At the end of the road, I came to a farm where cows grazed peacefully, but I did not stop there. Instead I entered the rows of trees bordering the river on the other side of the road. The river moved briskly over pebbles, and I imagined the water carrying you far, far away, as the stones in your pockets forced you to fall deep beneath it. It took three weeks for your body to come up again to the surface of the water, your body no longer burdened by the stones you placed in your pocket.

The world was at war. But still you dared to ask "how one's killed by a bomb. I've got it fairly vivid—the sensation; but can't see anything but suffocating nonentity following after" (D 5 326). It was because of the war you suffered from this "feeling of pressure, danger, horror" (D 5 313).

And so you took your life.

I so often think of Septimus. His shell-shocked words come to me today: "I went under the sea. I have been dead, and yet am not alive, but let me rest still" (MD 104). And so I wonder, Virginia Woolf, did you too ultimately long to rest beneath the sea?

Part II

"I think that our bodies are in truth naked. We are only lightly covered with buttoned cloth; and beneath these pavements are shells, bones, and silence."

The Waves 113

"The first—killing the Angel in the House—I think I solved. She died. But the second, telling the truth about my own experiences as a body, I do not think I solved. I doubt that any woman has solved it yet. The obstacles against her are still immensely powerful—and yet they are very difficult to define."

"Professions For Women" 241

Dear Virginia Woolf,

You said you succeeded in killing off the Angel in the House, but could never write of your body. It was just too difficult to do.

I still have not killed off that Angel in the House, that sweet girl who would like to float silently through rooms. How I wanted to stand invisibly over a life and simply heal someone. At five years old, I wanted to be Little Miss America with all my heart, and even entered the contest. I dreamt of the crown I would wear, the throne where I would sit.

You have helped me, Virginia, to see my life more clearly—to understand the legacy, the history of angels in houses passed from mothers to daughters so silently even the wind would not hear.

Dear Virginia Woolf,

Today, I will try and write of my body.

First, I want to write of the fresh smell of new life. I press my nose into my son's newborn skin and breathe in the scent of summer ponds and fields of flowers, and skinny-dipping bodies swimming, and lily pads moving slowly to the soft rippling.

It had taken three pregnancies to bring Max to life. At age forty-two, having a baby is no small task. It is difficult for me to tell the story of my first two pregnancies—how the embryos died an early death. At eight weeks, when I went to the doctors, all they could see was an empty sac with no heartbeat.

The embryos died, but the pregnancies continued on anyway. It was as if my body had played a rotten trick on me. The embryo was gone, but my breasts continued to swell; the morning nausea had started to set in, and the pregnancy fatigue made me long for sleep all day long.

Death had entered me and arrived, taking away those first few flickerings of life. Even with that sick, swelling feeling, I would bear no child. I wanted to wear black, to drape my life in mourning for what would never be. How could my body fail so miserably?

I was convinced that the first miscarriage was a lark, a fatal mistake. So many women have one, the doctors told me. It would never happen again to me. After the doctor removed the placenta and the remains of the dead embryo, I felt completely emptied out. It was as if winter had arrived early. The barren branches of trees were dying inside me, and the soil around me was dry, longing for water.

Dear Virginia Woolf,

When I first found out I was pregnant at the age of 39, I wanted to go out and celebrate my fertility. I knew I'd have no problem getting pregnant, I arrogantly thought. I looked forward to the eight-week sonogram, that first glimpse into the human life forming inside of me.

The doctor placed the sonogram receiver inside me, and all of our eyes stared at the screen. I couldn't wait to see what an eight-week embryo would look like. But waiting is exactly what we all did for a very long few minutes.

"Are you sure about your conception date?" The doctor leaned against a chair and folded his arms together. With his face so close to me, I could see the newly shaved stubs of his beard.

"Pretty sure . . . I guess my period can be irregular, so there could always be a mistake, but I don't think so." I spoke quickly, not even trying to hide the fear that was now there. I knew that first pregnancy test I took weeks ago had not lied.

"Well, I barely see anything there."

He was right. The black screen was certainly empty except for a miniscule ink dot.

"Let's take another pregnancy test. Maybe you're not even pregnant," he said cheerfully.

So I emptied some urine into a cup and left it there. Within a few minutes he came out and announced, No, you're pregnant all right. Perhaps you're just earlier on in your pregnancy than you thought."

"Do you think that's it? It's just that I got the dates mixed up. Though I really don't think I would. I mean I guess it's possible." The words didn't want to stop coming out of me.

"But most likely it's a miscarriage that's happened already."

I didn't want to leave the office. I wanted to stay there long enough for him to reverse his diagnosis.

He leaned his face close to mine and kissed my cheek. "We'll check you again in a few days, but it doesn't look good." And with those words, he took my chart and walked out of the door.

When I returned several days later, I dealt with my doctor's associates since he was out of town. A chubby man wearing a white jacket clicked the machine on and placed the sonogram receiver inside of me. We could see nothing except for that still black dot.

"Let me call in somebody to look at this," the doctor said.

A tall man with thick curly hair walked quickly into the room. He looked at the screen for only a second and announced confidently, "That's a blighted ovum. It's definitely a blighted ovum." He pointed his index finger to the screen, apparently delighting in the repetition of his findings. He then departed just as quickly as he had entered. In that moment I knew I was nothing more than a vagina holding a sonogram receiver lighting up an empty uterus.

Dear Virginia Woolf,

My first pregnancy was officially terminated in the doctor's office, while my second ended in an abortion clinic. I did not even know where I was heading on that wintry February day. I had switched to a fancy east-side OB, so I figured the procedure would be done in a comfortable place.

When Jeff and I entered what seemed to be a luxury building in the east 60s and told the security guard behind the desk the name of the office we were looking for, he just replied, "You don't have to tell anyone where you're going." I wondered why he said that as I passed by him.

The elevator opened up onto a stark waiting room. There was nothing in the room except for a few empty chairs and a young girl sitting behind a tall reception desk.

"I'm here to see Dr. S."

"Just sign in. I need the two hundred dollar fee for using the facility," she said brusquely. "Then we'll get to you when we're ready. "

Her harsh voice made me look once more around the waiting room. I felt like a criminal who didn't know why she had been incarcerated. Nothing hung from the walls. And the chairs were the simplest wooden hard-back ones, designed for ultimate discomfort.

A young black girl came off the elevator, had some words with the receptionist and then slumped into the hard-back wooden chair, her chin leaning sullenly into the palm of her hand. After a little while, I was given a thin, white cotton gown that had been washed but nevertheless looked worn.

"Go change into this in one of the bathrooms. Then you need to wait in a room just for you over there. Just stay there until the doctor comes." Her directions came at me quickly.

I knocked and opened a bathroom door. An Asian girl in her teens with a large, round belly stood by the sink. "Oh," she cried, startled by my sudden intrusion.

"I'm so sorry," I said and shut the door as quickly as possible. I had caught a glimpse into a sadness that was not meant for me to see.

My own grief had made my arms and legs heavy. I moved slowly despite my wish to hurry into my designated room.

Jeff was inside the room waiting for me. He sat on a bed with no sheet on it, across from another single bed with a limp, white sheet draped over it. Aside from these two beds and a single chair, the room contained nothing in it.

"Why do you think she sent me to an abortion clinic?" I was scared, but didn't want to admit it. This seemed like the kind of place where all sorts of botched up procedures could take place. We were not patients here, but criminals about to be sentenced in a courtroom of emptiness.

"I have no idea," he said nervously, crossing one leg over the other.

"I guess this bed is so I can rest on it after the procedure." I imagined prisons must have the very same type of bed.

My thoughts were interrupted when the anesthesiologist entered suddenly. He asked his routine questions and told me what to expect. As he sat across from me, I noticed how the edges of his pale green pants were stained with black grease. A slight rip had invaded the seams, causing some threads to unravel.

Once he left, the doctor who would perform the procedure entered. She was a sensual Greek woman with long, dark legs and arms.

"What am I doing in this depressing abortion clinic?"

"Yes, of course it's depressing. Everyone is here for some sad reason. There is nothing happy about these endings, regardless of the reason."

"But why did we have to do this procedure here?"

"Did you think you were going to be in a happy place? You are here for a sad reason. And so is everyone else here." She spoke to me as if the answers to my questions should be obvious to all.

Why was I being punished? And why were all the other women being punished as well? I wanted to know what our offenses were.

Fortunately, I fell asleep soon. As soon as the anesthesiologist's needle entered my arm, I was asleep. The bleeding that came after the D&C was not healing. I lay in bed, feeling the reams and reams of loss leaving my body.

Dear Virginia Woolf,

After my second miscarriage, death seemed to be everywhere. It was inside my body—barren, childless, a failure in every sense. And it was outside in the stillness of the winter air.

****

The last OB suggested it was time to see a fertility doctor. So Jeff and I entered another office where charts and articles about the benefits of fertility hormones were prominently displayed in notebooks and on walls. Everyone else in the waiting room sat with down-turned eyes. It was an unwritten rule that contact with a stranger could be perilous.

"Your problem," said the doctor in the most clinical voice, "is that your eggs are old."

His words made me sit silently, waiting for more bruising words that came in a cool, detached voice. He was a scientist, a researcher, after all, who was a practitioner as well. "By the time many women are forty, their fertility drops dramatically, and nine out of ten of their eggs are bad."

I felt like a crone. My hair suddenly turned gray, then white, and then finally fell out. And my skin became parched and wrinkled. Bags of skin puffed up beneath my eyes.

I had been sentenced as a crone. My eggs are old. My eggs are bad. His words rang like a nursery rhyme inside my head.

"At your age, every time you get pregnant, there's a fifty percent chance of miscarriage."

"What about the man? Is there ever anything wrong with him?"

"It's unlikely. Most early miscarriages are caused by egg problems."

I am old. I am old. I am a crone. It was so easy to start hating myself. The temptation was simply overwhelming.

"So what should we do?" Was there any solution he could offer me?

"It all comes down to a numbers game." Dr. G. leaned back in his chair; his hands were folded neatly on his desk, as he spoke. "You see, if one egg drops every month, and nine out of ten are bad, and when finally you get a good egg, all sorts of things could go wrong to prevent it from being fertilized. So, the point is to increase the number of eggs produced, in order to increase the chances of a good one."

"What about the risk of a multiple birth?" Jeff asked, nervously.

"In your case," Dr. G. said, and looked directly at me. "It won't be a problem. Multiple births occur when young women take fertility drugs. It's not an issue at your age. Your issue will be having a successful conception, and then pregnancy." Dr. G. spoke confidently in a medically neutral tone.

Dr. G. first conducted all sorts of tests—blood tests, urine tests, have sex and then come in and see me tests. Then he gave me a prescription for Clomid. It's one small pill a day for five days, but he warned me the month might feel like a long stretch of PMS mood swings.

"Come in the day you ovulate, and we'll do an IUI."

I needed to get used to the abbreviated fertility lingo.

Instead, I felt like a madwoman during that month on Clomid. Everything that bothered me, bothered me more. Everything that angered me, angered me more.

I am old, I am old, I am a crone, was all I could conclude.

Dear Virginia Woolf,

In between my first and second pregnancies, I saw an acupuncturist/herbalist who specialized in gynecology. Her goal was to get me pregnant. Min Lee was a beautiful Chinese woman with porcelain, clear skin, and long black hair. She checked my pulse, looked at my tongue, and then placed her needles throughout my body. But the main treatment would be herbs. From a long row of what looked like sticks and roots and crushed flowers, Min Lee scooped her shovel into nine or ten different herbs and made a special concoction for me. The directions for cooking these herbs were quite elaborate. First the herbs were soaked, then water was added and the herbs were cooked for an hour and a half; finally, these herbs were drained, put in another pot and cooked with additional water for another hour and a half. Min Lee had prescribed two cups of herbs per day—one cup in the morning and another in the evening. The drink tasted like a mixture of sticks and dirt.

"This will make you fertile," she explained. "It will take some time. But the herbs will work."

Her perfectly clear skin reassured me that this woman knew what she was doing. Besides she was a professor as well in the evenings at a local college out on Long Island. Each week I came to her, she stuck needles in my body, and I rested, drifting into dreams, as the needles tingled my skin. Then she gave me a fresh, new supply of her sticks and roots. "I am making this especially for you," she said, always smiling gently as she handed me the herbs in a paper bag.

The cooking herbs made the apartment stink of rancid soil. And suddenly my nose began to run, clogged up as it was with mucus. My chest felt drippy as well.

Min Lee stuck needles in my nose, treating me for a cold. But my symptoms only got worse. Only later, after the chronic congestion in my nose and throat went away, and Min Lee had accomplished her mission of getting me pregnant, would I realize how allergic I was to those herbs. Anyway, when my second pregnancy ended in miscarriage once again, I could only conclude that it certainly wasn't Min Lee's fault that my eggs were old.

Dear Virginia Woolf,

I diligently followed Dr. G.'s directions. On the morning of the IUI, I walked the five blocks to our car, drove back, doubled parked and then ran upstairs to get Jeff.

"Mission accomplished," he said, handing me the cup, as I walked into the apartment.

"Good going. But we gotta hurry now. It has to stay warm." Dr. G. had told me to keep the cup next to my body until I gave it to his receptionist. So, with the cup snuggled up next to my belly, I got into the passenger seat, while Jeff drove.

The twelve blocks to the doctor's office seemed to take forever. Each crag in the road, each jerk of the car, made me grasp the cup closer to my body. "I'm not going in there with you," Jeff said as we approached the wide expanse of Park Avenue. "I've done my part, and I just can't deal with it."

"That's okay." I kissed him on the cheek and with one hand beneath my shirt, I tightened my grip on the cup, while my other hand shut the door behind me. I waved good-bye, hurrying down steps, past a sign, Fertility Associates, in bold white letters set on a black background.

The door I had to pass through was not heavy to push. It let go easily. But once inside the office, I had to face a room full of women, most of them in their late thirties and early forties—women who flipped quickly through magazines, intent on appearing occupied as they waited. That morning I only glanced at the women. My attention was turned to the long counter of the receptionist. From beneath my shirt, I gingerly placed the cup on the black linoleum bordering the phone station. "Dr. G. said I should leave it with you," I said, trying to pretend I was calm.

"We'll be with you in a moment. We're quite busy right now." The receptionist called back to me. "Just stay where you are and wait right there."

My voice seemed to disrupt the silence that had settled over the room. I tried not to imagine everyone staring at me as I waited and waited by the counter, next to my very visible cup. I probably stood for only a few minutes, but it seemed like forever. I imagined everyone in the room peering through my clothes, undressing me slowly.

"Okay, come with me," the receptionist said officially. She took hold of the cup and led me into a smaller room with two nurses. The nurse directed me to write my name, then Jeff's, on a label placed carefully on the cup. "We'll be with you shortly," the nurse nodded dismissively, ordering me back to the waiting room.

The room was packed with women who chewed gum, crossed and uncrossed legs, their faces covered by the pages of magazines. In that waiting room there was always an eerie silence, interrupted only by a nurse calling out a woman's name. It was a silence bordered by the voices of the receptionists answering a constantly ringing phone. As women pushed and pulled the big black front door open and shut, the silence seemed to close up tightly too. In other moments it was as if the silence ascended to the ceiling, hovering invisibly over the heads of women, sitting and waiting.

"I went under the sea. I have been dead, and yet am not alive, but let me rest still" (MD 104). The words of the shell-shocked soldier came suddenly to me, soothing the emptiness of the moment.

Dear Virginia Woolf,

Today I write poems about the losses in my body.

Miscarriage

You must be
covered now
by moonlight,
and sleeping,
sleeping so peacefully
in starlight
sleeping
in a place where the dead
wait patiently
to become what is alive
once again

Hands

Small hands glide across the sky
    silently
        like stars meeting death

But it is birth I dream of—

Long ago the world was born
    from soil
        and the depths of ocean

The first people made from corn
    and water,
        the union of earth and sky

And now I dream of life—

Longing for small hands to form
    in the warm
        resting place of my body

Dear Virginia Woolf,

How did I end up believing that I could wait until I was forty without any problems? I figured a child would form easily, sliding out of the universe into my body. I had spent eight years of my late twenties and thirties in a library, getting a Ph.D. in English, and starting a career as a college professor. And then I didn't meet Jeff until I was already thirty-eight—love, coming finally to me later in life.

But then it happened suddenly—this longing for a child, like an ache spreading from head to bone and blood and kidney and liver and heart.

A lost child lives in the abandoned rooms of the body for a while before leaving for good. With each miscarriage, I tried to discern the moment of early death, feeling the presence, the enduring presence of life, the possibility, and then the emptiness like the branches of barren trees scraping my womb clean of the remnants of winter's dying.

Dear Virginia Woolf,

From Clomid, I graduated to Pergonal.

"The Clomid did nothing for you. It doesn't work for everyone. Maybe it has to do with your age," Dr. G. told me.

I am old, I am old, I am a crone. Each visit to the doctor's office brought with it new experiences of failure. And I was not alone. I sat among the tense career women packed into a small waiting room. Their eyes looked neither left nor right, but only straight ahead where no one else could catch a share of their glance.

Twice a day needles of hormones were shot into my butt, my thighs; the softer flesh was always best.

"Will it hurt?" I asked the nurse.

"Not too much. It feels like a bee sting."

Her words did not reassure me. And yet she was right. I pulled the syringe back, quickly stuck the needle into my skin and then slowly released the hormones into my body. For a moment, I felt stung and then it went away, and I felt nothing again. Jeff served as my necessary assistant, sanitizing the desk we worked on, mixing the drugs together and assembling the different parts of the needle together. After a while, we began to feel like experienced drug addicts.

We watched the video Dr. G. gave us several times. Nervously we meticulously followed the instructions, mixing the water and powder together to form the fertility solution, connecting the syringe to the needle and then filling it up with the Pergonal. That first time, Jeff got everything ready for me and then stubbed his finger with the needle.

"Remember, the drug's going into me, not you," I laughed nervously. A few drops of his blood fell onto the table, and we started all over again, first cleaning the table with rubbing alcohol and then my skin, as Jeff replaced the soiled needle before handing it all to me once more.

Every other day I needed to show up at Dr. G.'s office at 8 A.M. to have my ovaries monitored by sonogram—a job, I concluded, as I noted all the women jammed into his waiting room, that must be as boring as it is lucrative.

As the days progressed, my belly got round and bloated, filled up with the follicles of eggs stimulated into growth. I felt like a cat in heat, wanting to simply lie down and lick myself clean.

But there was no child. No pregnancy. No birth.

Dear Virginia Woolf,

My eggs are old. And that must be the fate of the crone. I diligently mixed the Pergonal, poured it into the syringe, stuck the needle into the fleshiest part of my butt, and pulled the handle back, inserting the hormones into me slowly, feeling the bee-sting sensation for just a few moments. As the month progressed, I could feel the eggs growing into little clusters inside my belly, like branches of trees unfolding into more and more stems, crowding the small space inside me.

I did everything I was told. I had sex when directed, brought the sperm in a plastic cup hugged against my belly, beneath my shirt, to Dr. G.'s office, where I placed it on the long counter, and stood there in the crowded waiting room, as the nurse routinely said, "Just a second. We'll be with you in a few minutes." As I stood, as if naked, with my precious cup, my back turned to the gathering of barren women, I could only ask as the moments ticked slowly by, how did I ever get into this situation.

My body had failed me.

Dear Virginia Woolf,

Once more your words come to me—how you succeeded in killing off the Angel in the House, that Victorian woman who glides selflessly through rooms, but you never could write of the body. Your words have new meaning for me as I remember those months going to Dr. G.'s office four or five times a week, sitting there at 8 A.M. with a room full of women, surrounded by a chilly silence. It is a silence that remains to this day over that humiliating period of time, a silence in my body that has not yet learned to speak.

Part III

"The past only comes back when the present runs so smoothly that it is like the sliding surface of a deep river. Then one sees through the surface to the depths . . . For the present when backed by the past is a thousand times deeper than the present when it presses so close that you can feel nothing else, when the film on the camera reaches only the eye . . . I write this partly in order to recover my sense of the present by getting the past to shadow this broken surface. Let me then, like a child advancing with bare feet into a cold river, descend again into that stream."

"A Sketch of the Past" 98

"Nobody sees anyone as he is, let alone an elderly lady sitting opposite a strange young man in a railway carriage. They see a whole—they see all sorts of things—they see themselves."

Jacob's Room 30-31

Dear Virginia Woolf,

Having a child enables me to see my own childhood through different lenses. Like a prism opening its multicolored light, I too journey there, backed by the past, and the present perceptions of new life resting in my arms.

In New York City, I look out of my window and imagine there is snow. I want to see the thick moist flakes falling from the sky, snow that covers the dirty sidewalks with a blanket of silence. I want to walk along the streets and feel the snow in my hair, thick flakes melting into long brown strands. The snow brings me deeper into other winters. But as I look out of my window, there is only a full gray; white smoke comes out of a chimney, and the buildings from my window block my view of the sky.

There is an emptiness when winter is about to approach—a dying that happens inside me each year, as I remember the winter many years ago when my father got into the old blue Dodge and drove away. I stood on the porch at thirteen years old as everything started to break inside me. I wanted to wave good-bye as he slowly backed out of the driveway and drove the car up the block, past Mrs. Nahemo's sheets hanging from the clothesline; past brown lawns sick with the season's dying. My mother stood several steps closer to my father than I. They barely spoke, except to say in terse and formal sentences: "Good-bye Bernie." "Good-bye Marilyn." Good-bye. Good-bye. Words uttered once, before their eyes looked sharply away.

My father only moved three miles away. I saw him two to three times a week, and we spoke at least once a day on the phone; and yet although I have always known where to find him, I spent many years of my life searching for my father.

Each year, as the trees become barren, I revisit the rooms of my childhood, and hear once more my favorite song repeating in my head, "Go tell Aunt Rhodie, go tell Aunt Rhodie, go tell Aunt Rhodie, the old gray goose is dead; the one she's been saving, the one she's been saving, the one she's been saving to make a feather bed."

Child of five, I hung my head down low from the swing as my feet stretched to touch the apple tree. I sang the refrain over and over again, wanting then to weep for the old gray goose dead and Aunt Rhodie on a rocking chair, waiting for death to seize the animal she would then stuff into pillows and chairs.

I grew then into the child of fourteen, staring out of windows with a yellow notebook in my hand. I liked to whisper the words printed on the cover: "Herald Square, University Notebook, Wire-O-Bound." A month before my brother David had taken the bus from Port Authority to go across the country, and then two weeks later my father left, too. One night he got into the blue Dodge and drove away to his new home in Main Street Flushing. My mother and I stood on the red brick stoop, watching the car inch its way into the road while my father whispered to me, "I'll see you Thursday," and then he glanced once at my mother. Neither one of them said a word as the car swerved suddenly out of the driveway, and my father glided past the Carbone and Nahemo households.

I liked to hold in my hands the wedding pictures taken twenty-four years ago; twenty-four, I repeated to myself, letting the sound of the number echo the loss of my father's leaving. In the wedding photograph, my mother did not wear white; she had no flowing gown. Instead large buttons started from below her neck and ran to her knees; the dress, fitted tightly about my mother's hips and waist, also stopped just beneath her knees. In the photograph, my father's arm rested stiffly across my mother's shoulders. They were young then, the perfect couple—my father just recently graduated from Harvard Law School, my mother, a youthful beauty with black curly hair highlighting the softness of her face. Their eyes looked innocently towards the future, towards the years and years in front of them—years that would easily unravel joyfully.

Twenty-four years later, just weeks before my father moved away, my mother stood silently at the top of the second floor staircase of our house, her hair splintered into many threads, while the evening light hovered round her. She stood on the staircase mutely, listening, as my father shouted from the bottom of the stairs, "You ruined my life" and then she echoed the very same words to him. "You ruined my life." Her words tumbled and rolled over the worn blue and white spotted carpet covering the staircase, and then she turned away and entered the bathroom, her tears suddenly muffled beneath the larger sounds of the water from the faucet filling up her bath.

In the twenty-four years they were together, I had rarely seen them reach for one another affectionately, had hardly ever seen them touch. I turned the pages of the wedding album and found the honeymoon images: my mother by the water, in a boat, the oars by one side as she laughed girlishly, while my father's mouth moved up into his cheek to ever so slightly suggest a smile.

But my brother David had predicted it all. "The nuclear family is falling apart. It's a dead relic of the past," he told me as he sat on the brown swivel chair in the music room. A few weeks before, David had taken me to the Student Action Committee to End the War in Vietnam. He introduced me to his friend Jonathan as his little sister who had the potential to really do something one day.

After my brother and then my father left, I would sneak into the city alone every Saturday to go to the Student Action Committee to End the War in Vietnam. I told my mother I was visiting a friend, but instead of going several blocks away, I walked up to the bus stop at the intersection where Gable's Inn Pizza Place, the Blue Sea Diner, Fashion Barn, and Mobil gas station met.

Once inside the bus, I gazed out at the passing buildings: the low thatched roof of Carvel, where a large, plastic brown bonnet ice-cream turned round and round; rows and rows of identical red brick houses were connected by a silver fence and white banisters. The last stop of the bus was Main Street Flushing—Main Street Flushing where Gertz and Kleins Department stores stood side by side.

When I arrived at Main Street Flushing, I entered my favorite place, the corner cigar shop and bought several packs of sugarless gum. In twenty minutes, I could chew an entire pack, spit it out, and start on another one, as I boarded the number seven train and sat back on my seat while Bliss Street, Lowery Place, and Junction Boulevard went by. At Queensboro Plaza, I crossed the platform, and whether I got there in the morning or evening, it did not matter, because it was always dark there. Rain often drizzled down onto the tracks, as I waited for the RR train to appear, with its white lights invading the space where I stood.

At Astor Place, I came out of the subway and walked towards Washington Square Park, past the men in a corner playing chess, past a fat man selling balloons and bearded men sleeping on benches, until after a few blocks I arrived at the Student Action Committee to End the War in Vietnam. I was greeted warmly by a young woman who sat me down at a desk and gave me hundreds of flyers with the words boldly printed, OUT NOW. U.S. OUT NOW. March on Washington, April 24.

And so after my father left, going only several miles away to Main Street Flushing, I spent most Saturdays sneaking into the city, so I could stuff anti-war leaflets into envelopes.

Dear Virginia Woolf,

I revisit now the landscape of my childhood, that time my family fell suddenly apart, and the specter of the Vietnam War seemed to border it all. Over our piano, where I had once played *Fur Elise*, my brother had taped a poster of the My Lai Massacre. Women and children gunned down to the ground. The blood flowed over their bodies, blood covered the ground where they lay, and the contorted faces of the survivors, their screams, disturbed the eerie silence of our house, and continue to be a presence even now, as I recall easily the horror of that time.

After my father moved away, I would often meet him twice a week at his apartment near Main Street Flushing; there one small window overlooked a courtyard and down below children played stickball all summer long and through the start of winter. They played until the frost formed, and with the cold came the quiet my father so desperately sought.

My father would pace his apartment in the evenings. Like a clock ticking in the morning, waking the sleeper out of his dreams, forcing him into the harsh world of concrete objects, my father would step upon those wooden floors, wondering why everything had gone so suddenly wrong.

A photograph of Harvard Law School hung above the threaded couch, reminding him always of his graduation twenty-five years ago. The other side of the room was barren except for a white wall with thin antennas from the television.

A white line of boric acid separated the three-foot entranceway from the living room. "It's the demarcation line where no roaches can cross," my father would explain.

In the evenings a woman walked along the floors of her upstairs apartment in high-heeled shoes that created a thumping sound, repeating and reaching down into my father's living room. Most evenings he'd get a broom and turn it upside down so he could bang on the walls to get her to take off her shoes. Eventually he dented the ceiling with his rage.

In the evening, on the television screen, together we could see the scarred and bleeding bodies of men, women and children lying in fields. Planes flew over the barren fields that had died from the bombs we Americans had dropped from the sky.

"When is this country going to learn anything?" my father asked, as the screen switched from the dead and dying bodies in Vietnam, back to America where police in riot gear dispersed the thousands of students with tear gas. The students shouted, "Out Now. Out Now. U.S. Out Now." First a stone fell, then a rock hurtled across the sky, and more bodies ran to escape the men with helmets and guns.

"When is this country going to stop?" my father's voice rose in exasperation. "You see the subways for yourself, how we crunch together like sardines. But it's that way because nobody does anything to change it."

I thought of David on his way to California to organize against the war. I imagined him making his way up the block, walking farther and farther away from our worn two columned house, as he sang silently to himself, I am leaving, I am leaving, I am leaving them all behind.

David left the paint peeling from the white two columns of our house. I used to like to sit in the living room and stare at the green rug torn at its edges; above the fake fireplace hung a painting of hills and trees enclosed in an imitation gold frame. On another wall I could find a painting of a man hunched over to his knees, his back bending naturally into his cane.

My father's words became a singsong melody, repeating in my head like the songs I sang as a girl playing jump rope and hopscotch:

> You fight with the subway
> You fight with the bus,
> And then you come home,
> And fight with your wife.

One night, before my father moved away, as I stood by our long, golden-colored curtains folding naturally around a wall of windows, he called to me: "Are you taking everything down now? Are you writing it down, so you'll have notes when you grow up and become a writer."

I appreciated his encouragement. In a yellow Wire-o-Bound notebook, I jotted down overwritten descriptions of houses and trees. When my father left, my writing became even more fragmented. I tried to record the last Thanksgiving Day Dinner at Sokol's Delicatessen. I sat with my mother and father, (David was already away), as the waiter brought us hot open turkey sandwiches at the deli. The creamy mashed potatoes covered with thick brown gravy only made that last meal even more tasteless. From my seat I could see past the glass door, outside to the number thirteen bus stop, just a few hundred feet away from the deli.

Soon after my father left, men named Arthur, Bob, and Harold would arrive at our door. Some came in convertibles; others had shiny black shoes, ties and sports jackets. Most were balding middle-aged men with rounded bellies sticking out over their belts. My mother had gone from her parents' house into marriage, and so after almost twenty-four years, she found herself, unhappily, for the first time, quite alone.

I hated the night sounds that can fill an empty house: the dripping of water, the clanging of pipes—I heard all of this as I sat at our white linoleum kitchen table long after my mother had gone to sleep.

Dear Virginia Woolf,

I can hear your prophetic words: "Unless we can think peace into existence we—not this one body in this one bed but millions of bodies yet to be born—will lie in the same darkness and hear the same death rattle overhead" ("Thoughts of Peace" 173). Your words connect a childhood bordered by the Vietnam War to the terror of September 11, and my present life as a mother.

But today I want to revisit the landscape of my childhood. At the Student Action Committee to End the War in Vietnam, I met Jonathan, who at eighteen seemed worldly compared to my fourteen years of existence. Jonathan had thick, bushy, brown hair growing wildly up from his head. He came from a faraway place in Queens called Far Rockaway. I would often see him at demonstrations in Washington Square Park. Out of the thousands present, somehow we would always find each other, and then afterwards walk together around the village, where we passed the men sleeping on park benches. Many had black beards, stray hairs grown over faces. The scent of alcohol wafted up into the air as I passed by them. And there were old women too, sifting through garbage cans for food.

One afternoon it began to drizzle as we walked. Rain streaked down abandoned buildings; drops clung to windows and the branches of trees bordering Washington Square Park. Jonathan wore a nylon blue raincoat fitted loosely over denim pants, while I let the rain fall on my hair and darken the faded pink T-shirt. Slivers of rain sprinkled the buildings of New York University, fogged up the glass swinging doors of the Loeb Student Center where I had gone for large meetings urging the students to fill the park across the street with their demands: "Out Now. Out Now. U.S. Out Now."

"I don't know if you really understand what we're doing here. If there's a revolution, blood's gonna run through these streets. It's no game we're talking about. The rich ain't gonna give up what they got without a fight." Jonathan was more than an anti-war activist. He was a socialist as well. Jonathan always walked even more quickly when he spoke, as if his words seemed to animate movement.

I listened quietly, excited about the idea of a revolution, and change, and people rising up to make a different world. As we passed the chess players huddled over their tables, a young unshaven guy with thin, straggly hair and dirt smeared all over his dungarees came up to us.

"Hey, you got any change?"

"Here, take a quarter." Jonathan dug into his pant's pocket for the coin. "Panhandling. I bet he's making a small pile of money today. It's easier to do than a lot of other things."

"How much do you think he gets?"

"Oh, I'd say he's pulling in five or six bucks an hour at the rate he's going. It sure beats working your butt off at McDonald's. I'll tell you that much."

We moved through the white arch where people circled round a woman with a guitar. She sang of wind and flowers.

"Hey, you know I've never even seen where you live. Why don't we go hang out there for awhile?"

I had only met Jonathan at the Student Action Committee, or found him at a demonstration in the park. In the year that we had become friends, we had never even spoken on the phone. I didn't even know Jonathan's address or phone number.

"Okay. I'll take you there."

Together we rode the subways to Main Street Flushing, then took the number thirteen bus, past Gertz and Kleins, past Carvel's brown bonnet twirling with ease, past the red bricked attached houses, and then finally past Woolworths, until we got off at the intersection where Gable's Inn Pizza Place, the Blue Sea Diner, Fashion Barn, and Mobil gas station met.

"You know, I've always wondered where you live." Jonathan looked up at the wide expanse of sky, and the dusk slowly descending over us, as we walked the four blocks to my house.

We climbed the red brick stoop leading to my home and entered without knocking after I slipped the key inside the door and turned the knob quietly. First I called to my mother, but when no one replied, I announced nervously, "Guess no one's home."

Jonathan followed behind me, stepping slowly.

In the corner of the living room, my cello leaned against the wall— that pear-shaped instrument I had wrapped my arms around, my small fingers searching for notes down its long curvaceous body.

"Hey, let's hear some tunes." Jonathan sat himself down on our stiff, upright chair, waiting for the music to begin.

"What should I play?"

"Anything. Anything at all will be just fine."

I played a Chopin sonata I had practiced over and over again. Those melodies spoke to me of old women on busses leaning against windows, their skin grown soft, their breasts sagged downward into the folds of bellies. The music made me know dying did not call, but entered unannounced.

When I finished playing, Jonathan had moved from the chair to the floor, several inches away from me. He looked up at me and clapped. "Bravo. That was beautiful."

"It was?" Most people considered the sounds of my music to be scratchy at best. The awkward and tentative notes were like my fourteen-year-old body, part woman, but still mostly child. The hips were starting to round, but my breasts were still two barely formed nubs of flesh not knowing where to go.

"Why don't you show me your house?" Jonathan's voice had become suddenly soft-spoken.

We climbed the blue and white carpeted stairs. Jonathan moved obediently behind me as I stepped quickly, wanting to stay ahead of him.

The walls in my room were violet. When I was little, the walls had been pink; and the tiles on the floor were thin rivers of pastel colors: blues, purples, and yellows blended together. I would sit, cross-legged, staring into the patterns of light there, singing, "Go tell Aunt Rhodie, Go tell Aunt Rhodie, Go tell Aunt Rhodie, the old gray goose is dead. The one she's been saving, the one she's been saving, the one she's been saving to make a feather bed."

Jonathan plopped down my bed and leaned his back against the wall. I sat myself next to him.

"Pretty nice place."

"You think so?"

"Hell yeah. You should see where I live."

I suddenly became aware of my loose brown corduroy pants, those hand-me-downs from my older brother. My newly formed hips filled in the baggy parts that were made for the tall, lanky bodies of boys. Sitting there, with my mostly child body that was changing slowly, I felt fat.

For so long I had waited impatiently for each demonstration in the city to happen, because there, in the crowd, Jonathan would always pop up, like a Jack-in-the-Box, never failing to appear. Suddenly in the midst of thousands, I'd spot him, his bushy brown hair blown wildly by the wind. In between demonstrations, I'd make up conversations in my mind with Jonathan, telling him about the day my father drove away, and the journey I would take almost every Saturday on the number thirteen bus to Main Street Flushing, where trains would take me down to the Student Action Committee to End the War in Vietnam.

But when Jonathan pulled me towards him, and I landed with my head snuggled against his arms, I felt nothing then, as though all feeling had simply disappeared, and there was only emptiness remaining where his wet kisses entered my mouth. I felt nothing as his hands stroked the nubs of breasts waiting to be formed beneath my faded pink T-shirt. His hands moved quickly down my legs, stopping only to unzip the hand-me-down corduroy pants, his fingers exploring deep inside me; but still I felt nothing.

So this is sex, I thought. This is what my parents argued about behind the door of their bedroom.

In Jonathan's arms, I could rest from the harsh voices of my parents, voices wrestling through many long nights in bitter arguments, continuing on, long after my father had moved away.

"I gotta go," Jonathan whispered.

"I know." I smoothed the loose corduroy pants down into place before tucking in my faded T-shirt. "I'll walk you to the bus stop."

"Good plan."

Jonathan's arms dangled down his side, while I folded my hands beneath my chest, embracing my childlike body moving downstairs. The melodies of old women seemed to move through the house, hovering in the living room around the painting of a frail man bent down low into his cane.

Outside the street lamps hummed into the night. Jonathan walked quickly, his legs liked to bounce along the pavement, while I felt my feet fold cautiously round the sidewalk.

"How long will it take you to get home from here?"

"A couple a hours. I live all the way on the other side of things."

"I guess the bus oughta be here soon." I was trying to fill the silence with some words. We both stared for a moment at the thin mannequin in a plaid bikini standing in the window of Fashion Barn.

"Man, am I gonna be busy soon. Took the GED last month, and now I'm starting Borough of Manhattan Community College next month. Course they'll teach me a bunch of lies there, but I'm ready for 'em this time. Know what I mean?"

"Yeah." I was only half listening.

"At least science ain't like history. They'll have to teach me some straight facts instead a warping the story."

"Yeah, that's true." I found myself saying the words Jonathan would like to hear.

When the number thirteen bus finally came, Jonathan kissed me on the cheek and ran quickly inside. "Be good," he turned to me before dropping his coins into the hands of the bus driver.

I nodded okay. I will be good. I will be better than good. I longed to be a shadow standing over a life, invisibly caring for all that had been broken. But Jonathan was now far away. So I turned from the intersection, glanced quickly at the thin mannequin in Fashion Barn's window, and made my way back to my home. Those four blocks were a path leading me into the many days that I had spent staring out of the windows of my room with my yellow Wire-O-Bound Notebook. I had looked at the snow falling on the cracked and dry soil of the backyard, wanting then to capture the silence of those winter afternoons that bordered the emptiness of many leavings.

When I got back to the house, there was still no one home. There were only those house sounds—the clanging of pipes, the dripping of faucets, the humming of wood.

In my room, I slipped off my corduroy pants and T-shirt. The clothes fell from the chair, where I had thrown them, onto the pastel tiled floor. The brown and pink materials blended easily into the blue, green and yellow colors of my floor.

I stared at my body in the mirror, stared at the faint nubs of breasts barely beginning to form, at my round belly, my widening hips—my body, still the body of a child. And I hated what I saw. I was fat, I told myself. The mirror did not, could not lie.

I slipped a T-shirt over my body and climbed slowly into my bed, all the time wishing Jonathan was still there with me. I could still feel his hands sliding down my legs, as the house sounds reminded me I was alone. Pipes clanked intermittently while water dripped from the bathroom faucet, drip, drip, dripping, all the way from downstairs.

The angry voices of my parents interrupted the beginnings of sleep. "I'll tell them everything. I'll tell them every damn thing when they're twenty-one," my father shouted.

I curled my legs and arms up into my belly, waiting for my mother to respond, but there was only silence and the humming of the house sounds that bordered my dreams.

"I'll take this weekend, and you'll take the next, and then we'll fight it out about who will get the last week-end of the year." My father's voice reached me from the solitary rooms of sleep.

I moved from left to right and right to left, all night long, moving to the rhythm of voices in my dreams, and then there were long stretches of quiet when I slept fitfully, feeling only the stillness of abandoned rooms.

Several weeks later, I saw Jonathan once more at the Student Mobilization Committee to End the War in Vietnam, and then the war ended shortly afterwards, and I waited fourteen more years before I would accidentally bump into him again.

Dear Virginia Woolf,

Today I think about your soldier, Septimus. He could only speak with stops and starts, his language shattered by war; and Septimus longed to drown, to lie deep beneath the sea, to die once more to find his lost friend Evan, blown up into a million pieces by the bombs of World War I.

War bordered my childhood. It was always in the background, silently defining a moment. I enter once more the music room where I played *Fur Elise* during the long afternoons of summer. There my brother hung a poster of the My Lai Massacre; those faces of women returned to me, have never left me—blood mixed with tears streamed down their cheeks contorted by unutterable grief—the dead bodies in a pile gunned down behind them. What did it mean to be a survivor, I wonder as those images re-enter my mind.

When someone speaks to Septimus, words become shells falling from a plane. His entire conception of time has new meaning for him: "the word 'time' split its husk, poured its riches over him; and from his lips fell like shells, like shavings from a plane; without his making them hard, white, imperishable words, and flew to attach themselves in an ode to Time; an immortal ode to Time" (MD 53). Septimus sings and hears his dead friend Evan's answer from behind a tree, from that timeless place he stands, "among the orchids."

The pictures from the past stand still today. And the words that bring life to what is now gone, become, as you say, Virginia Woolf, "an immortal ode to Time"(53).

First there was one miscarriage, and then there were two, and then my father got sick and died. Like a frame in a movie, I still see him getting into his old Dodge and driving just several miles away to his new home in Main Street Flushing, as I stood on the stoop by my mother, wishing I could run behind the car and bring them back together.

"I'm not afraid of death," my father told me twenty-five years later, a man grown suddenly old from the tumor in his head. "I was in World War II, you know. I'm not afraid to die. I knew then it could happen any time. We said, if the bullet had your name on it, it was your turn to go."

Like a movie, my father's life unravels in my mind today. There was something he wanted to leave me with, as the illness transformed his trim body into a swollen mass of heavy flesh expanding. "It goes so fast," he said, resting after his struggle to learn once more to walk. "Please, please, just enjoy it."

On another day he lay on a bed unable to lift himself up.

"I feel like the Tin Man."

"Why?" I asked, sitting beside him.

"Because he didn't have a brain either."

Is death an empty room? When I was pregnant, I would often dream of my father, who died just three days before Max was conceived. I would dream of solitary rooms and polyurethaned floors—the shades half drawn, and then I'd wake to the fluttery movements of my little son growing inside me—little ripples against my belly like hiccups or wishes being blown from bubbles.

Death is a closed door, where, on the other side, the dead remain. We cannot see them, but they are near, looking, listening, watching over us invisibly.

Part IV

"I need a little language such as lovers use, words of one syllable such as children speak when they come into the room and find their mother sewing and pick up some scrap of bright wool, a feather, or a shred of chintz. I need a howl; a cry."

The Waves 295

Dear Virginia Woolf,

My son was conceived first outside my body, in a small dish and then inserted in me along with three other embryos. I have pictures of the five cells clustered together, a wet mass of bubbles unfolding.

From IUS's, I graduated to IVF.

As I pumped more and more hormones into my body, my father lay dying. His head and body swelled up from the growth in his brain. As I frantically ran to Dr. G.'s office each morning, with the eggs growing quickly in clusters inside my belly, my father slipped into delirium. I remember his last words so clearly.

"I won. I beat the cancer. I beat it all." And with that declaration, my father became unconscious, blending easily with sleep.

The day after his funeral, the eggs were extracted, and then three days later, the embryos were implanted.

My son's life was the gift my father gave me, from that nameless country where he now dwelled.

*****

As the months progressed, I could feel Max's fluttery movements. My mother said her babies felt like butterflies opening inside her.

*****

Where does life come from? Do we emerge from the stars? From the mixing of darkness and light?

During my pregnancy, my attention turned inward, as life slowed down quite a bit. Sun, moon, and rain seemed to border my days, as I entered that space between sleep and waking.

Dear Virginia Woolf,

But after three years of trying, a life from the faraway reaches of the deeps and depths of the universe had finally, finally formed inside of me.

*****

I pick up a baby book that explains the fetus is in a space capsule traveling through primordial time in his mother's body as he journeys to his birth. My body feels suddenly linked to the cosmos. The origins of life in my body—sea salt and brine—the oceans moving in me.

The "ghostlier demarcation" of life that was once old is now forming anew.* The secret of origins, mystery of water—all that resides in me now as I move through the day with my son growing inside me.

* "Ghostlier demarcations" is from "The Idea of Order at Key West" by Wallace Stevens.

Dear Virginia Woolf,

I can hear your words: "The birds sat still save that they flicked their heads sharply from side to side. Now they paused in their song as if glutted with sound, as if the fullness of midday had gorged them" (*The Waves* 165).

Where does life come from? Out of nothing comes first one cell, then more, then a small beating heart.

Our mother's bodies are our first homes, where sea and sky blend beautifully together, for we all must take our "voyage over a sky dark like polished whalebone" (146).

We all start off in the warmth of water, and then spend the rest of our lives longing to be near the ocean or sea.

Dear Virginia Woolf,

How does one write of the mystery of the body, the stories the body longs to tell?

For the first twenty weeks of my pregnancy, I threw up every day—in my car, in my office at work, after a class I was teaching. Those hormones I had pumped into me were still reacting in my body. And then quite suddenly the nausea disappeared, and I could feel the baby hopping like a small frog inside of me.

How does one write of birth, of death, without cloaking it in all sorts of cliches?

*****

I could see a small, upright hand in the imprint of the sonogram. Hello, from the womb, he seemed to be saying.

We were two heartbeats then in one body, soon to be severed dramatically by birth.

Dear Virginia Woolf,

Today I want to write of birth, of the secrets held in my body.

*****

"Honey, I got to tell ya. You don't look like you're in labor to me. I'm sure we'll be sending you home. You'd be a lot more uncomfortable, and I mean a lot more, if this was real labor," the night duty OB nurse said to me. Her face was like a ripened pear with soft wrinkles and a double chin.

"When you're in so much pain, you can't speak, then it's real. Then come back to me."

It was the habitual 3 A.M. false labor run to the hospital. I was back home by 4 A.M., and fell into a deep sleep. Contractions, like menstrual cramps, kept coming all day.

By 3 P.M., I was in the OB's office, responding to his call to come right over. "Let's induce the labor now, since you might go through a few more days of this," he urged. "Otherwise, you'll end up totally wiped out before the real thing starts." He wanted me to go straight to the hospital, where he'd meet me. "Jeff can bring your stuff. Tell him he doesn't have to hurry over. Checking in will take some time."

It was strange to be sitting alone in the maternity waiting room of the hospital. I could hear a woman moaning loudly—her pain sounded as if it came from some dark cavern of the earth.

A thin and very worn looking black man ran up to the nurses' station. "Somebody better get my wife some medication. She's in agony," he yelled. "Somebody better do something to help her."

"We're working on it," a young nurse replied politely.

"It's just not fair. Nobody's doing anything to help her. Can't you hear what she's going through?"

"We're working on it."

The dull moaning remained constant, and then its pitch increased until the one woman sounded more like a chorus of women weeping for the ancient wounds of the earth.

Somebody told me she was having post-birth contractions. It never occurred to me that such a condition could exist. I figured if I got through the birth, I wouldn't have to worry about any more physical pain.

"That's just not true, honey," this same somebody gently replied.

The head OB nurse behind the circular nurses' station suddenly called out to me. "What are you doing here? You don't seem like you're in labor to me."

"It's being induced. I've been having false labor since 3 A.M."

"Oh." She paused for a few long moments. "I say go to Central Park and walk for two hours. That'll bring it on. Then you'll know what real labor is."

"Anyway, you should at least go take a walk while you're waiting. Go over and see the nursery or something."

So I waddled over to see the newborns with the red/pinkish, wrinkled skin sleeping, sleeping so peacefully. And then I went downstairs and bought sugarless banana and chocolate lollipops and fruity ice pops for the labor. Even though I was only in the hospital shop, I felt like I was in a maternity boutique trying to pick out just the right items for my journey.

So first Jeff got there, and then the doctor arrived, and then the drug Pitocin dripped into me slowly. The labor started out with mini volcanoes that became more intense until it felt like large pieces of granite were exploding into fire in the farthest reaches of my body. And then for a moment it was quiet before the fire raged on again uncontrollably. I was constantly pleading for more drugs, and the nurses would threaten to wheel me into the emergency room for a C-section if I didn't keep working.

When they told me it was time to push, I felt relieved because it meant the fire would stop burning inside me. As I pushed, it seemed the baby was coming out of my butt, ripping, splitting something open, until he flew suddenly out of me. I could see him propelled quickly out of my body, all wet and rubbery, moving into the doctor's arms at a fast velocity.

When Max was brought to me, I felt a sense of quiet like the moments after a rainfall. The silence was drizzling down, down, down, to cover us. Curled up in my arms, he looked around and made soft purring sounds. The nurse placed his mouth on the nipple of my breast. He sucked for a few minutes, and then my breast fell out of his mouth, and I just lay there, holding him.

Dear Virginia Woolf,

Your character so beautifully says, "I am no longer January, May or any other season, but am all spun to a fine thread round the cradle, wrapping in a cocoon of my own blood the delicate limbs of my baby" (*The Waves* 172).

Becoming a mother had made me more forgiving of my own parents. Past and present exist in a violet prism where one blends imperceptibly into the other.

*****

I am no longer just a daughter, reliving the wounds of the past. I wade through those same streets in Queens, this time both mother and daughter simultaneously.

Part V

"Mine is a gloom like a mist that comes and goes."

Vol 2 Diary 237

"Strong emotion must leave its trace; and it is only a question of discovering how we can get ourselves again attached to it, so that we shall be able to live our lives through from the start."

"A Sketch of the Past" 67

Dear Virginia Woolf,

Your famous words come back to me today: "For we think back through our mothers if we are women" (AROO 79). But how do I write of my mother? How do I find words for her? There are images—a lovely woman walks through rooms. Her dark hair curls beneath her neck. And then the image goes blank and I wonder does she wear shoes, or is she barefoot? No, she is no earth-mother, though she is certainly fertile. My mother always wore cheap shoes that ate her toes away. All that remains is a yellow crumbly substance. But except for her feet, my mother has always been admired for her beauty.

I think today of Mrs. Ramsay, because reading *To the Lighthouse* helped me to understand my mother more.

There is some secret Mrs. Ramsay knows—it has to do with the sound the sea makes as she sits in the evening sewing quietly with eight children running about, the sea, like a mother, calls out to her—I am your comfort. "I am your support" (TL 16). But then the sound the sea makes changes suddenly. Waves are no longer lullabies. Waves crash about reminding Mrs. Ramsay of the destruction of the land, and she awakes from her quiet reverie, startled by her own terror.

It is the same with my own mother. In a moment my mother's victorious laughter, her face creased with smiles, would change suddenly—just when it seemed no one was looking; and then my mother would grow old all at once. The flesh beneath her eyes would become soft like goldfish, and roots of wrinkles would form from the sides of her mouth. My mother would seem strangely alone, and like Mrs. Ramsay, far, far, out to sea. But then suddenly, in another moment, all would change, and my mother would be young again, surrounded by the fabulous sensations of a party.

There are secrets my mother has kept, a legacy of violence passed down by each succeeding generation of women. My great-grandmother raped and murdered in that old land called Russia, drowned in a river by Cossacks; and then my grandmother, now motherless, coming to this country at age sixteen, married at seventeen, and with child shortly afterwards. No wonder my mother was always afraid of the dark.

Dear Virginia Woolf,

Today I think of Lily Briscoe standing at her easel in *To the Light-house*, wanting to find a form for her loss, for the dead Mrs. Ramsay who would come no more. Yes, I can see Lily at her easel, dipping her brush into the paint, dipping, tunneling into memory. Lily, symbolic daughter, spinster lady/artist. . . . Lily on the beach, finally with the realization, "In the midst of chaos there was shape; this eternal passing and flowing (she looked at the clouds going and the leaves shaking) was struck into stability. Life stand still here, Mrs. Ramsay said. 'Mrs. Ramsay! Mrs. Ramsay!' she repeated. She owed it all to her" (TL 161).

And the tears streamed down Lily's face, as she longed for the dead woman to appear. Mrs. Ramsay, that beautiful angelic woman, who believed all women should marry, should have children. It was silly of Lily to be a spinster and an artist. Silly Lily, she would say.

And yet Mrs. Ramsay was still Lily's muse.

You said, Virginia, you had to kill off the Angel in the House in order to write. And you did just that. With a turn of the page, Mrs. Ramsay is gone, dead, and Lily is left with her paints and the memory of the woman who could not, and did not know her.

This Angel in the House still lives inside me. Like a phantom in the dark, she silences my writing, telling me, oh, no, you shouldn't say that. It wouldn't be nice. Someone might be offended. She watches over me, telling me to float gracefully and invisibly through rooms.

You have helped me, Virginia, to understand my own demons—to identify the voice of the angel, who would like to kill any self apart from her.

And in my mother's beauty, I see Mrs. Ramsay, that lovely woman everyone always admired when she entered a room. And yet when she was alone, away from the spectacular noises of one of her dinner parties or the demands of all those children, Mrs. Ramsay would feel she was far, far, out in the sea, where the waves might bury her forever.

Like Lily Briscoe, I have wanted to lay my head on my mother's knee and simply rest there.

Dear Virginia Woolf,

The skin on my mother's face is soft like the petals of roses. Even as an old woman, my mother is still lovely. Becoming a mother has made me need my own mother in a new way. Who else is there who wants to listen to every nuance of my son's routine and regimented day?—the way he burped, and cooed and pooped and sucked, and meandered through the park holding my hand for balance, as he sought to teach himself how to walk.

In these sleepless nights where day blends easily into dusk, I feel as though I am journeying through the history of my mother's body.

Dear Virginia Woolf,

In those weeks following Max's birth, where day and night reversed itself, and sleeping and waking became indistinguishable states, I found that, frame by frame, the movie reel of my childhood played on for me.

My mother was always afraid of the dark. On Friday evenings, even before my father had moved away, just when dusk had slipped into night, my brother would meet her at Andre's Beauty Salon, where Andre, a thin and graceful French man with a gift with combs, would carefully tease her hair up, up, up on top of her head, and then fold it into beehive layers with a round brush and hairspray. David would arrive promptly at seven and walk beside her those five blocks back to our home. By the time they entered the house, the Good Humor Ice Cream Man and his truck had already left after selling all of his eclairs and ices. The whiffle ball games had ended, and there were no children outside playing hide and seek.

After my father left, my mother would go out on a date some nights. I remember once when a black sleek convertible pulled up to the house and a man in a sports-coat, no tie, just an opened shirt that allowed the hair from his chest to peek out, knocked on the door to our house. I watched as my mother came down the stairs in a simple black dress, a string of pearls, and a beauty that could hypnotize anyone. The destination for this date was the racetrack. My mother introduced me to the man in a red paisley shirt, and I mumbled a perfunctory hello.

Alone in the house, I spent the evening doing homework, listening to music, and then staring out at the bright lights in the kitchen, as the familiar house sounds of pipes rattling kept me company. Outside the cars occasionally swished by. Several hours later, my mother returned. Her date had lost quite a bit of money that night, and not surprisingly we never heard from him again.

My favorite of her dates was a man named Arthur. He was a balding man with a small pouch of a stomach, who had managed to retain his good looks. Arthur always came to our door with many praises. He thought my mother was simply a fabulous woman, and I, her daughter, deserved the same compliments. I think I could live with this guy, I figured. But one day Arthur showed up, and explained to my mother that he had been separated from his wife and was going to try and work it out with her. So we never saw him again either.

Dear Virginia Woolf,

I remember so clearly the first summer after my parent's winter divorce. I went to music and art camp, and hugged my pear-shaped cello close to me, as if the scratchy sounds I created spoke of all that had suddenly failed. My father had moved several miles away to Main Street Flushing, and soon afterwards introduced me to his new girlfriend, while my mother struggled to keep the dating going. She went to middle-aged single nights at the local Queens and Long Island clubs, and drove up, while I was away at camp, for a singles' weekend in the Catskills.

It was at the pool, in the Catskills, during a weekend for the mature and middle-aged, that my mother met Mordecai, a recent widower, whose wife had died suddenly in her sleep. After several weeks of dating, my mother asked Mordecai if he would like to drive her to see her daughter on camp visiting day. In a letter, my mother wrote to tell me she would not be coming up alone.

That summer I played the cello in the afternoons; holding the large instrument between my legs, I could only hope the awkward, scratchy sounds would eventually mature into the voice of sea and wind..

When the day came for my mother's visit, I suddenly became overwhelmed with the desire to simply hide. Although I knew I should sit on my bunk steps, as I looked out at the cows nibbling from green and brown fields, and waited for my mother to appear, my legs carried me elsewhere. I scurried, like a squirrel, into the woods, walking on a path of leaves soaked by the summer rain of yesterday. I walked and walked, going farther and farther away from the bunk steps where my mother might be waiting for me, until I could no longer enjoy the shade of the woods, that haven of trees blocking the entrance of the sun.

As I walked I remembered our last Thanksgiving together, right before my father moved away to an apartment near Main Street Flushing. The rain pounding onto the ground as we ate our late afternoon dinner seemed to announce the breakup of my family.

"Next year, you can all come to my apartment," my father said. "And even you, Marilyn, even you will be invited there." My father spoke and then took a bite of the tasteless hot open turkey sandwich.

There were few people eating their Thanksgiving meal in Sokol's Delicatessen that afternoon. A waiter with greased back, black hair, whose hands smelled of sour pickles, took our order and delivered our food to us.

Several weeks later, when my father moved into his apartment in Flushing, the meals with my mother in our Queens home seemed equally drab. We would sit around our white linoleum table, talking in soft, barely audible tones. Sometimes my mother would clean up the dinner quickly and then get ready for the evening's activity. Perfumed and powdered, with her hair tightly teased into a beehive resting on her head, my mother would emerge from her bedroom and answer the door. A man equally oiled and pruned would enter the house, and after a few introductory words, the two of them would descend down the red-bricked stoop, past the green and brown front lawn, and into his sedan.

In the evenings, I would take my cello from its green plastic covering; those scratchy sounds and awkward melodies seemed to express all that I had no words yet to say.

The past returned easily to me, as I walked along the campgrounds that first summer after my parents' divorce. I journeyed over the events of the past year, wanting to understand why and how my family had so suddenly fallen apart. I figured I'd better return to the bunk stoop, or my mother would search the entire place for me. So I retraced my steps slowly, reluctantly forcing my legs to take me where I did not want to go. When I came out of the woods, I found my mother by the bunk with a short and skinny old man with long curly hair and a pocketbook draped down his shoulder. A round and shiny medallion dangled from a chain clasped around his neck. He looked like a senior member of the TV show, Mod Squad.

"There you are. We've been looking all over for you." My mother clasped her arms around me, pressing me close to her. I wanted her arms to remain with me just a little while more, but soon she was pointing excitedly to the odd little man standing beside her.

"I'd like you to meet my friend, Mordecai," my mother smiled triumphantly, her mouth opening like a rose, petal by petal, until the smile was her entire face; and her eyes seemed to wink at me gleefully, as if to say, you see, you see, I got a man, a man, to drive me to see my daughter.

Dear Virginia Woolf,

As Mordecai came around our house in Queens more and more often, and my mother would open the door, clothed in a black dress and
pearls, her hair sprayed into a beehive, her mouth a bouquet of smiles, I
began to get nervous. I started to think of some way to prevent a marriage I could see was bound to happen.

One afternoon I was on a Greyhound bus headed for Albany to visit
my best friend from camp. A tall and clean-shaven man sat next to me,
his large head propped against the window. While I sat upright, and he
leaned, as though for extra energy, against the window, we took in the
scenes of New York City; first the yellow dingy walls of Port Authority
Bus Terminal, where the revolving doors went round and round, and
faces entered. When the bus left the terminal, the gray sky seemed to
hover over the burnt out buildings west of Ninth avenue; and then suddenly there were malls, and gas tanks, and Newark Airport, bordering
the wide and listless lanes of the Jersey Turnpike.

"Where you off to all by yourself?" The tall man asked.

"I'm visiting my best friend."

"A best friend," he paused. "It's a great thing to have a best friend."

I thought to myself, this tall man seemed wise.

"Yeah. I can tell her anything. We write to each other all the time
and share everything. And I mean everything."

"Well, then. You'll probably be friends forever." He turned once
more to look out the window. "I tell you, there's nothing like a good
friend. There really is nothing like it." His face was next to mine, and I
could smell the cigarettes in his breath.

"Yeah," I said slowly. "I know what you mean."

"You know. You're a great kid. It's too bad you're just a kid, cause
I really do like talking to you. Too bad you don't have a double of you
who is all grown up."

"Well, I do have a mother. And she is divorced. And," I added
proudly, "She is a lot like me. But just older."

"You have a mother who's divorced," he said slowly, as if to turn
this information over on his tongue.

"I think you'd like each other. Especially since me and my mother
are so similar."

"Well, if your mother is like you, I'll certainly like her. He took out
a pen and piece of paper. "Okay. Okay." He seemed to like the sound of

his voice repeating itself. "I'm going to give your mother a call when I get back home."

And with those words we parted.

When I first told my mother about the man I had found for her to meet, she was startled that I had taken on the role of matchmaker. But then she came around. "Okay, I'll meet him. But first I better let Mordecai know about this."

That evening I overheard my mother on the phone. "Yes, Rachel met this man on a bus, and she really liked him a lot, and it turns out she gave him my phone number, and he's going to call."

I could hear the awkward silence on the other end of the phone.

"I just figured I should tell you about it," my mother said.

But three days later when the tall and clean-shaven man I had met on the bus called to speak to my mother, everything had changed, and by then, my mother was already engaged to be married to Mordecai.

Dear Virginia Woolf,

The day I had been fearing finally came—the day when my mother announced in a grand and victorious voice that she would be getting married.

"He's so different from your father," she whispered. "That's why I know it will work."

I did not understand how my mother could marry a small man of 108 pounds, with a goatee and long gray curly hair. How could she marry a man who carried a brown, leather pocketbook and wore a shiny, ceramic medallion down his shirt that unbuttoned just enough to let the graying hairs of his chest stick out? Fifteen years older than my 48-year-old mother, his mod appearance was discordantly mixed in with another look that signaled the onset of old age.

After they married, we moved into his Central Park West apartment. From the long palatial windows in his living room, I could see the great expanse of the Park unfolding into meadows and trees.

Before dinner, Mordecai would sit by his long windows, slowly sipping martinis, while my mother sat across from him with a glass of white wine, her beehive hair teased up and sprayed like a thinly made bird's nest. The light at dusk entered that white-carpeted room; the light spread over a marble coffee table and created shadows on the high-backed Victorian chairs where they sat with their drinks. I figured all rich people must have martinis before dinner and then afterwards get comfortable with a bottle of dark port wine.

At fourteen years old, I had tried everything I possibly could to prevent my mother from getting married to Mordecai, but the more I tried, the more inevitable the marriage became.

Dear Virginia Woolf,

Now many years later, I wade easily through those awkward adolescent years, those years bordered by war. It came to us in the living room, through the television images of men gunned down and bombs and mines exploding. Legs and limbs torn apart, flying haphazardly about—all this surrounded the reality that my family was falling apart. And when my mother first remarried, and then my father too, and we moved away from Queens into my new stepfather's apartment on Central Park West, I would lie awake at night hearing the screams of women and children gunned down; their cries invaded that time before sleep would come and dreams would cease.

Shortly after my mother remarried, the war finally ended. After school, I would shut myself up in my room and listen to Joni Mitchell's "Blue" album over and over again; lying in my bed, I could wander with her mournful voice over the contours of my new room. And when I wasn't listening to Joni, I was journeying through the dimly lit streets of Dostoevsky's novels, longing to visit Russia and kiss the Motherland, that place my entire family left so many years ago.

I revisit easily the second summer after my parent's divorce. At fifteen years old, I can see myself then in dark, blue dungarees and a white T-shirt snugly covering me. My thin hair, light brown mixed with streaks of childhood blonde, fell down my back. I wanted my body to grow backwards, grow down into a little girl with thin legs and a flat chest. I wanted to stop the hips from curving, the breasts from growing.

Several years later, when the onset of young womanhood had taken firm root, and we had left Manhattan to live in a house, I would make my way up the block wearing a silk flowered dress, and without my knowing it, Mordecai would peek out of the window, lifting the blinds up in the morning to catch a sight of me, moving slowly away from him.

Dear Virginia Woolf,

 Often at night as I lay in my bed, I felt frightened. While my mother slept deeply in the room down the hall, her new husband would stay up late listening to modern and classical music, as he slowly sipped glass after glass of port wine. The discordant sounds—the notes from violins and violas speeding up suddenly in a high-pitched frenzy of terror before slowing down into the drugged forgetfulness of sleep and dreams—made me toss and turn with fear. The screeching, nightmarish music seemed to uncover a reality obscured by the daylight.

 It was during that time I first read *Mrs. Dalloway*. At sixteen, I did not understand a word of it. I only knew the words seemed to dance across the page. And then the words were my body, and I was dancing, as I lay there feeling the movement of language down my arms and legs, knowing what I could not comprehend was something I loved deeply nonetheless.

 Now after all these years, as I try to reconnect with my younger self, I know for sure it was books that saved me.

Dear Virginia Woolf,

I wanted my body to disappear. Like you, I did not like looking in mirrors. During the second summer after my parents' divorce, when I was fifteen years old, and my mother was already remarried, and we had moved away from Queens to an apartment on Central Park West, I went upstate to visit my friend Beth at Somerstock.

When my friend Beth laughed, her large body shook, creating movements trailing behind the giggle in her voice. We held hands as she showed me the grounds—the outside stage surrounded by empty chairs waiting for an audience. The green and dying brown grass circled round bushes huddled together, secluded from the tall oak trees towering over the stage.

I sat and watched Beth rehearse—she sang, she danced, she clowned around on stage; and then after a couple of hours I walked around the place by myself, since she was still busy. I was happy to be away from home. Mordecai had let me know he didn't want me around. At sixty-three years old, why would he want to deal with a teenage girl, anyway, he had told me. He'd already been through that twice, and it was enough. At least I could converse peacefully with the trees, bowing their heads low that afternoon to listen patiently to the silence in me.

"Hey Beth's friend, Rachel," a voice interrupted the quiet of the trees. "Do you mind if I walk with you?"

Beth had already introduced me to Dan, one of the Somerstock teachers, who was suddenly by my side walking with me.

"Sure. Why not?"

"How long you visiting here for?"

"Just a couple of days."

"That's nice. I come here every summer to help direct the plays. It's a good break from the high school teaching I do during the year."

We entered the woods, where the light from outside seemed to wane naturally, blending into the dark barks of trees.

"I'm in high school myself."

"Oh yeah. What grade would that be?

"I'll be starting tenth grade in the fall."

Dan listens to me. First, he tells me he is divorced. He has a ten-year old daughter. Then I tell him about the day my father drove away in the old Dodge to Main Street Flushing. I tell him about my mother's remarriage and the new apartment we are all suddenly living in together.

"That must have been so hard for you to have your parents get divorced." His dark beard seemed to crawl sadly along his face

"Well, in the beginning it's bad. But then after awhile, you get used to it."

"I hope so. I worry about my little daughter. I just want her to be okay."

"She'll be all right. Take it from me. Don't I seem okay?"

"Talking to you sure makes me feel better," Dan said.

For awhile we were silent, and then Dan began to speak again.

"You know, you also could be my daughter. I'm certainly old enough to be your father. But you'll be my friend instead. And I'm glad, because you're really very special."

I wanted him to continue saying nice things about me. My legs seemed to pick up speed with his words, my legs stepping lightly upon the twigs and soil.

The light from the late afternoon had already begun to disappear into evening.

"Let's get out of these woods." Dan led. And I followed. We stepped up large wooden planked stairs. Clop, clop, clop . . . my feet were noisy. Dan opened the screen door with plenty of openings for the mosquitoes to enter his room.

"I never met anyone like you. You're just so very special."

"Really?"

"Yeah, really. I just wish you weren't so very young." He stroked my arms with the tips of his fingers. "Well . . ." I paused for a moment. "How old are you?"

"Thirty-five," he whispered.

He was twenty full years older than I, and that seemed so very, very old to me.

"You, see, tomorrow my girlfriend will come visit me. She's not at all like you. We don't even have all that much in common. But still, Rachel, the two of us could never be together. You're just too young." His voice grew fainter and fainter as he spoke.

"You're like a little friend to me. A little friend I just want to hold."

Dan's words made me feel he really cared about me. For so long, so much had been breaking inside me. He thought I was special and wanted to be my friend.

When he kissed me, the hairs from his beard scratched my face. I was relieved he didn't find my fifteen-year-old body awkward or ugly.

"Come lie down next to me." Dan pulled me closer to him. And for a moment, we lay next to each other. I could hear myself breathing while slender rays of light from the moon lit up a corner of his room.

At first I wanted to be held. So when Dan wrapped his arms round my back, and his fingers crawled up my shirt, and found my breasts, for a moment I felt comforted; and then there was nothing but an emptiness, a numbness.

"You're really so very special," he repeated over and over again. "But remember, tomorrow, my girlfriend will come, and we won't be able to get together anymore."

I wanted to go home, to be far away, to be once more invisible, someone without a body.

"I gotta go," I whispered finally. The words were short staccato sounds cutting into the air, moving against the darkness.

"Let me look at you once more," he said and stroked my arms as I shook quietly. I placed my white T-shirt over my head and picked up my red cardigan sweater from the floor, draping it over my shoulders.

"Remember, tomorrow," Dan said as I got up to leave. The screen door hit the wood several times, making a banging sound that accompanied my movements down stairs into the darkness.

When I got back to Beth's room, she popped up from her bed immediately. "Are you okay?"

"Yeah, I'm fine."

"Are you sure?"

"Yeah," I could hear my voice tremble slightly.

"I was worried about you."

"No. I'm okay. Really I am." I went into the bathroom and took off all my clothes. The water from the shower soon streamed down me. I scrubbed my legs, moved up to my breasts and rubbed and rubbed with the washcloth, wanting to melt the soft parts of me down into the rest of my body.

Part VI

"Behind the cotton wool is hidden a pattern; that we—I mean all human beings—are connected with this; that the whole world is a work of art; that we are parts of the work of art. Hamlet or a Beethoven quartet is the truth about this vast mass that we call the world. But there is no Shakespeare, there is no Beethoven; certainly and emphatically there is no God; we are the words; we are the music; we are the thing itself."

"A Sketch of the Past" 72

Dear Virginia Woolf,

At just a few days old, my little son first bites my breasts, gumming the nipple hungrily, greedily; the sharp pains of his grasp make me wince. But then he soon learns to suck with more ease. I do not have much milk, but the little I do have, I give him. In my arms, he sleeps, resting deeply from his long journey.

No one told me it would be so physical—this young life nestled against my breasts, this new life fitting snugly in the pockets of my chest.

Dear Virginia Woolf,

I went there, Virginia, across the ocean to the University of Sussex, where you live in the dusty photocopied remnants of notebooks the librarian brings out for me—notebooks stored in vaulted rooms, housed down creaky stairs where so many women have stepped—women whose lives have been mainly unrecorded, unnoticed, and disregarded.

So I came to the place where your papers are guarded by librarians with thin wired glasses and white hair, their lives spent protecting the words you left us, words that continue to resonate long after your death. Today, one sentence, in particular, keeps repeating in my mind: "As a woman, I have no country. As a woman I want no country. As a woman my country is the whole world" (TG 109). The aging librarian brought me three large envelopes filled with copies of your notes for *Three Guineas*, your pacifist manifesto that rages against the barbarism of war abroad and the humiliation of women in the home.

Years before, I had held in my hands an original draft of *To the Lighthouse*, as I sat one day in a small research room of the New York Public Library. I stared at the barely perceptible jagged lines of handwriting running together, and then I could make out some words that spoke of sea and sand, an island of women—whale-boned, moon-dipped images of lighthouses. I held all this in my hands, and trembled. Only pencils could be used by those lucky enough to handle these original papers. If someone even dared to take out a pen, suddenly behind doors, librarians would run, ready to swoop down and tackle the haughty criminal.

In the library in Sussex, an older man sat across from me, his head bending into papers, his glasses falling down the incline of his nose. In a corner of the room, a younger, but middle-aged woman in a neat, starched, white blouse and long cotton red skirt sat at a microfiche machine viewing documents. These people have spent their lives in libraries, I thought, noticing how their faces sagged ever so slightly downward, their eyes weary from use. Every once in a while the old man grabbed his pencil to write furiously in his notebook.

Outside the sun warmed the fields and buildings. I wondered what am I doing inside on such a day, but then in another moment, I realized that I have never been happier. And so, like the old man across from me, I opened one envelope and bent my head into the copies of the notebooks.

I find a scrapbook of articles all recording the beliefs of the early twentieth century, the idea that "women can't write, women can't paint," women can't think, women are like children and savages, women's development has been arrested. And as the 1930s progressed, you moved from recording the injustices against women to the cruelty, the overwhelming cruelty of Nazis.

Dear Virginia Woolf,

On another day in Sussex, as I strolled through your lush gardens—reds, greens, blues, and the purples of flowers growing without restraint or fear, I could sense the beauty that you so longed to record. I stepped lightly over stones, and sat without fatigue on a bench in the midst of all this life—roots and petals, stems and seeds—all had survived the ravages of war.

As I write this, I can connect once more to my own younger self, hidden beneath layers of selves we outgrow but never discard. I think of you, Virginia, as a fifteen-year old girl. You described yourself as a broken moth, a not-yet butterfly. I can hear your words, "the blow, the second blow of death, struck on me; tremulous, filmy eyed as I was, with my wings still creased, sitting there on the edge of my broken chrysalis" ("A Sketch" 64).

I imagine you, Virginia, in that Victorian room of yours, motherless at only thirteen; and then there was the second blow just two years later, the death of your half-sister, Stella, the death following her return from a honeymoon—yes, death claimed her, too. And there you were, Virginia, like a broken butterfly, your wings creased, unable to fly, on the edge of a thick, milky cocoon.

You dipped your pen deep into the past to write of all that loss, and the silent abuses of the heart.

Dear Virginia Woolf,

In Sussex, I sit outside on the grass, near your writing room, and long to see my father once more. I want the dead to rise up from the ground to be with me once more. The day is like a painting waiting to be finished. Light rests on fields of green and skinny trees bending low to the whims of the wind.

So I call out to my father, call to him as if he lived now in the round bushes growing in the fields, or in the two large oak trees that border the windows of your study. And suddenly he is right there, right before me, sitting in a wooden chair, as if my longing could actually wake the dead.

My father looks tired from his journey. "Please, please," he says once more to me. "You must enjoy it. It goes so fast." And with those words, he disappears into the sunlight and shadows dancing there.

Dear Virginia Woolf,

You longed for water, for death by drowning. Your journals before you died reveal how the war was present everywhere around you: "Now we are in the war. England is being attacked. I got this feeling for the first time yesterday. The feeling of pressure, danger, horror. Vita rang up at 6 to say she cdn't come. She was sitting at S(issinghurst)t. The bombs were falling round the house. They'd been fighting all day. I'm too jaded to give the feeling—of talking to someone who might be killed any moment" (D 5 313-4).

No, bombs do not fall in New York City. But after so many lives are gone, I feel my own vulnerability. Nothing will ever be the same. My son's bubbles wafting up in the air only remind me that something has gone dead, yet I am still alive. Each time I drive over a bridge, I hope I will live to return back over it.

Dear Virginia Woolf,

It is the one-year anniversary of 9/11. None of us have ever been so carefree again. That day still exists in my memory, like the dead do, invisibly behind a closed door. Have we all become broken in this past year, all of us longing to repair what is now invisible, but apparent to none but ourselves? It is only now I understand something has been breaking all year long.

*****

I can hear your words, "Yes, the chimneys and the coast-guard unseen by any one make one remember the overpowering sorrow. And what can this sorrow be?" (JR 49). And then you answer your own question: "It is brewed by the earth itself. It comes from the houses on the coast. We start transparent, and then the cloud thickens. All history backs our pane of glass. To escape is vain" (JR 49). I understand now that as children we are transparent, but as we grow we inherit the violent history of the earth.

And then, of course, there is the sorrow "brewed by the earth," the sorrow of all those lives lost in the many phases and manifestations of war.

Dear Virginia Woolf,

It is Septimus I long for, as I stroll along the New York City streets where everything looks the same, but beneath the surface, we have all been irrevocably changed. Septimus, who feels "this gradual drawing together of everything to one centre before his eyes, as if some horror had come almost to the surface and was about to burst into flames" (MD 21).

We have never stopped mourning the loss of all those lives. It is difficult to stand away from New York City and watch the skyline. I cannot bear to look at what is no longer there. Those brash towers, symbolizing the center of a city, of a people's psyche, unafraid to build higher and higher, feeling always the rush of invulnerability.

All that is certainly gone.

As Septimus sits on a park bench in London "the world wavered and quivered and threatened to burst into flames" (MD 21).

Were you Virginia, some prophet, peering into the terrors of the next century?

Dear Virginia Woolf,

I can hear your words: "This moment is composed of a sense that the legs of the chair are sinking through the centre of the earth, passing through the rich garden earth; they sink, weighted down. Then the sky loses its colour perceptibly and a star here and there makes a paint of light. Then changes, unseen in the day coming in succession seem to make an order evident" ("The Moment" 4).

We are women without countries, women without borders, women who wander the earth seeking to discern the form of a moment, as we journey through memory.

As I read your words, I feel my own feet sink deep into the earth, into the past that lies buried there.

Works Cited

Stevens, Wallace. *Collected Poems*. New York; Knopf, 2002.

Woolf, Virginia. *A Room of One's Own*. New York: Harcourt Brace Jovanovich, 1929.

———. "A Sketch of the Past." *Moments of Being*. Ed. Jeanne Schulkind. New York: Harcourt Brace Jovanovich, 1978.

———. *The Diary of Virginia Woolf*. Ed. Anne Olivier Bell. 5 vols. New York: Harcourt Brace Jovanovich, 1977-84.

———. *Jacob's Room*. New York: Harcourt Brace Jovanovich, 1922.

———. *The Moment and Other Essays.* New York: Harcourt Brace Jovanovich, 1948.

———. *Mrs. Dalloway*. New York: Harcourt Brace Jovanovich, 1925.

———. "On Not Knowing Greek." *The Common Reader*. First Series. New York: Harcourt Brace Jovanovich, 1925.

———. "Professions for Women." *The Death of the Moth*. New York: Harcourt Brace Jovanovich, 1942.

———. "Thoughts of Peace in an Air-Raid." *Collected Essays*. Vol. IV. New York: Harcourt Brace Jovanovich, 1967.

———. *Three Guineas*. New York: Harcourt Brace Jovanovich, 1938.

———. *To the Lighthouse*. New York: Harcourt Brace Jovanovich, 1927.

———. *The Waves*. New York; Harcourt Brace Jovanovich, 1959.

About the Author

L isa Williams is Associate Professor of Literature at Ramapo College of New Jersey, where she teaches writing, literature, and women's studies. She is the author of *The Artist As Outsider in the Novels of Toni Morrison and Virginia Woolf*. Her essays and reviews have appeared in such publications as *Women's Studies Quarterly, Virginia Woolf Miscellany*, and *Transformations: A Resource for Curriculum Transformation and Scholarship*. Her poetry has appeared in *For She is the Tree of Life: Grandmothers Through the Eyes of Women Writers* and *Bubbe Meishahs by Shayneh Meidelahs*. She lives in New York City with her husband and son.